The Power
Of Positive Desire

By

Joe F. Hernandez

The Power of Positive Desire
ISBN 0-9667225-0-7
Copyright © 2000 by Joe F. Hernandez
811 Woodmeadow Place
Oakley, CA 94561

Editorial Consultant: Cynthia Hansen
Cover Design: Greg Lane, Inspired Graphics
Text Design: Lisa Simpson, Words Unlimited

Printed in the United States of America.

Contents

Introduction

Is it wrong to desire to *do* something, *have* something, or *be* someone for the glory of God?

I am writing this book because God wants you to know it *isn't* wrong to desire to progress or to prosper in life. It isn't wrong to desire to produce fruit for the Kingdom of God or to be promoted to successful living. Jesus came so we could have more abundant life (John 10:10). Therefore, we were born to desire and enjoy just that!

When Jesus was born, the angels said, *"Glory to God in the highest, and on earth peace, good will* [desire] *toward men"* (Luke 2:14). The angels' words reflect God's desire for us to experience only good.

Therefore, if you desire what is holy, right, and good, it is God's desire being expressed in you. Think about it — why would it be wrong for you to desire what Jesus has already provided for you? Jesus restored to you the good life, and it's right for you to desire what is already yours!

When most of us think of desire, we think of evil desires. For instance, King Ahab desired wrong things. He and Queen Jezebel were evil in their desire to take Naboth's vineyard from him. King David also acted on an evil desire when he lusted after Bathsheba and killed her husband so he could have her for his own. Finally, Judas acted on an evil desire when he chose thirty pieces of silver in exchange for his betrayal of the Lord. Bad choice!

Since the day God created Adam and Eve in an environment of abundance, health, happiness, and fulfillment, His plan has never changed. He wants us to desire His plan for our lives. We were born to live in God's desire of abundance and happiness.

We have a capacity no other creature in God's creation possesses. No flower, tree, bird, fish, animal, ocean, mountain, river, planet, or star has the ability or power we have. In fact, not even the angels possess our capacity to ponder, to plan, to think, to dream, to believe, to achieve, and to desire.

It is not wrong for us to desire anything from God as long as we stay within His boundaries. We have no business even asking for something outside of the Word of God. That is an example of *negative* desire.

When I was a little boy, I lived with my grandmother. She used to tell me, "Don't go past the hump in the road, Joe, or you'll get into trouble." The hump in the road was about a house and a half away from her home. Grandma didn't tell me that because she wanted to keep me from enjoying life. She just loved me and didn't want me to get hurt. She didn't want evil to overcome me.

In the same way, our Heavenly Father doesn't want us to leave behind the boundaries of His Word. If we go past the perimeter or fence of His Word, we will get into trouble. It isn't that God wants to keep us from enjoying life; He just doesn't want us to get hurt. He wants us to stay inside the fence of His Word so the devil doesn't devour us.

So let's explore the power that is unleashed through positive, godly desire. That power is the divine force that opens the door to God's highest and best in our lives!

Joe F. Hernandez

CHAPTER 1

The Positive Desire Of Abraham

We can learn a great deal about desire by looking at the life of Abraham. If Abraham were alive today, some people would accuse him of trying to control God. They would say that Abraham was trying to tell God what to do. But consider this: Did Abraham come up with the plan to make a covenant with God all by himself? Or did he just believe in the covenant God had chosen to make with him?

Abraham just desired to have what God had previously promised him. He actually laid claim to possess what God had already given him.

It was God's desire to enter into a covenant with Abraham. God is the One who first thought of it. He is the One who first wanted it. Abraham just hooked up with God and was therefore privileged to take hold of this new desire for his life.

Act in Faith on God's Desire For You

If Abraham had listened to religion, he never would have received the blessings of God. He might have surrendered God's dream and believed that he could never dare try to inherit something he didn't have and didn't deserve. Instead, Abraham would probably have just asked God to give him patience and strength to bear his burdens.

It was God's desire to multiply Abraham's possessions and make him rich, but Abraham had to do his part. It was God's will to give Abraham his heart's desire — a son — and to make him the father of many nations, but Abraham still had to do his part. Even though God gave these promises to Abraham, Abraham had to act on his own desire and believe he had received those promises by faith before he saw them manifested in his life.

The Heavenly Father is the same yesterday, today, and forever. Therefore, He will not force His desire on us just because He wants to bless us. He gave us His Word just as He gave it to Abraham. He will only bring His desires or His promises to pass in our lives as we desire them ourselves and then act on them in faith.

But realize this: Once you decide to accept God's desire and act on it, there will always be people who tell you not to get your hopes up. "Just settle for mediocrity," they will say. "Accept your sour situation, and don't expect it to change. Don't even think about the impossible."

You know, Abraham probably heard this same type of unbelief from his own friends and relatives. He probably heard advice like, "Give up. What's the use? You are not able to bear a son at your age. You will never receive God's promise."

Our Father is waiting for us to do what Abraham did. He wants us to believe His Word in spite of our contradicting circumstances. He wants us to desire His Word for our lives enough to *act* on it in faith. He wants us to take full advantage of His desire to bless us so that, together as the Body of Christ, we *amaze* the unbelievers. He wants us to be so convinced of His blessings that we forget our natural limitations and start acting on the Word!

Desire Within the Boundaries Of God's Word

God wants us to pursue our desires, but they must always be in line with *His* desires for us. First John 5:14,15 makes this point very clear:

1 JOHN 5:14,15
14 And this is the confidence that we have in him, that if we ask any thing according to his WILL, he heareth us:
15 And if we know that he hear us, whatsoever we ask, we know that we have the petitions that we desired of him.

The word "will" in this verse actually means *desire.* So we could read it like this: "If we ask anything according to God's *desire*, He hears us."

There are certain things for which we shouldn't even ask. For instance, if a man asks the Father for another man's wife, the Father won't even hear that request. Why? Because His Word forbids it. The man is asking for something outside the fence of the Word and the desire of God.

Likewise, if a young lady asks for God's permission to marry a man who isn't committed to God, she is asking outside the boundaries of God's desire or will.

What about a man who wants a new boat so he can spend every Sunday out on the lake? That man has wrong motives for his request; therefore, he is asking outside the boundaries of God.

When I was a boy, some of my deviant friends would tell me, "Ask your grandma if you can do this or that." If the activity they were encouraging me to do was wrong, I would automatically know not even to ask. I'd just tell my friends that my grandma wouldn't let me.

My friends would say, "How do you know she won't let you if you never ask?"

I'd respond, "Well, I just know that there are some things you don't even ask."

Similarly, there are some things you should already know not to ask the Heavenly Father. For instance, don't ask, "Lord, can I cheat on my taxes?" You already know the answer.

And don't ask, "Lord, can I skip on paying my tithes this time?" You already know the answer.

"Lord, can I hate my brother and walk in unforgiveness?" You already know the answer.

"Lord, can I kill my neighbor?" You already know the answer.

"Lord, can I have my neighbor's wife?" You already know the answer.

We have no business even asking for something that is outside of God's Word. There is nothing wrong with us asking for and receiving things from God, but our requests must be within His boundaries.

If you want a wife, God wants you to have your own wife and not someone else's wife. If you want a husband, God wants you to have one who is committed to Him. If you want a boat, He wants you to have one to use *His* way, and that doesn't include always missing church. You have to ask within the boundaries of His Word.

MARK 14:36 (*NKJV*)
36 And He said, "Abba, Father, all things are possible for You. Take this cup away from Me; nevertheless, not what I will [desire], but what You will [desire]."

Bring your desire to a new, higher level. Desire *God's* desire for you. He wants you to desire. His will is for you to desire. He waits for you to desire. T. L. Osborne said, "One of the most vital truths that you will ever discover is that God wants you to have good things in life — the best in life, but he must wait, until you desire, before he can give them to you."[1]

PSALM 37:4
4 Delight thyself also in the Lord; and he shall give thee the desires of thine heart.

What do you delight in? Do you delight in "R-rated" movies? Do you delight in the internet? Do you delight in worldly magazines and worldly music? Do you delight in pornography? Do you delight in secular television and radio? Or do you delight yourself in the Lord?

Make God's heart and His desire yours. If you haven't been delighting yourself in Him, start now. As you do, He will give you the desires of your heart.

PSALM 37:5
5 Commit thy way unto the Lord; trust also in him; and he shall bring it to pass.

---

[1] T. L. Osborn, *Go for It! Get the Best Out of Life* (Tulsa: Osborn Books, 1983), 79.

There are three divine guidelines in this verse you must remember to follow. First, you have to delight yourself in the Lord. Second, you have to commit your way to Him. Third, you have to trust in Him. As you delight in Him, commit your way to Him, and trust in Him, your desire becomes what He desires. This is when He will bring your desires to pass.

God Fulfills the Desires
Of Those Who Fear Him

Psalm 145:19 gives us another important qualification that we must meet so God can pour out His blessings on our lives:

PSALM 145:19
19 He will fulfil the desire of them that fear him: he also will hear their cry, and will save them.

What does it mean to fear God? It means that you are continually aware of His presence and that you respect what He is thinking about your situation. You are aware that He is watching and that He sees and knows every move you make.

When you forget about God, it's easy to act as if He isn't watching. But when you remember He is always watching, it helps keep you from getting involved in a lot of things that would displease Him.

To fear the Lord means that you are aware He is always in the room with you. For instance, when I was a boy, my grandmother used to tell me, "Don't eat anything because we're getting ready to eat dinner." If I knew she was in the room, I never considered going for the food. But when Grandma was out of the room, I'd take a peak out of the corner of my eye to make sure she wasn't watching. Then I'd check to make sure she was somewhere else in the house. If I knew the coast was clear, I'd move in for the steal and find something good to eat — usually sweet!

When I did this, I wasn't respecting Grandma's word nor her authority. I wasn't reverencing her or fearing her displeasure. But all that changed when I knew she was watching. With Grandma's eyes on me, I did indeed respect her word and fear her displeasure!

The same thing is true with God the Father. If we stay continually aware of the fact that He is watching us, we will much more readily respect His Word and His authority. We will have a reverent fear of displeasing Him and therefore keep away from things He forbids.

You might think, *No one is watching; I wonder if I should click on to this pornography website? I wonder if I should I steal this money from my company? I wonder if should cheat on my spouse?* But just because your pastor, boss, spouse, or brother in the Lord isn't nearby, that doesn't mean the Lord isn't watching.

To fear God means you are aware He is watching when no one else is around. If you go to the highest mountain, He sees you. If you go to the lowest valley, He sees you. If you go up in a plane, He sees you. If you go down in a submarine, He sees you. If you climb up in a tree, He sees you. You can run from God, but you can't hide. To fear the Lord means that you purposely reverence what He told you and you purposely stay aware that He is watching you.

PROVERBS 10:24
24 The fear of the wicked, it shall come upon him: but the desire of the righteous shall be granted.

PROVERBS 11:23
23 The desire of the righteous is only good: but the expectation of the wicked is wrath.

When you *delight in the Lord*, when you *are committed to the Lord*, when you *trust in the Lord*, and when you *walk in the fear of the Lord*, you desire only what is good. You are the righteousness of God in Christ. You never desire what is wrong or bad; you only desire what is right and good according to the Word of God.

You don't desire sexual abuse; you desire holy matrimony. You don't desire drugs to get you high; you desire the anointing of God on your life. You don't desire to vandalize; you desire to help rebuild your community. You don't desire rebellion; you desire to live as a law-abiding citizen. You don't desire worldly music; you desire to worship and praise your Maker. You don't desire worldly dancing; you desire to celebrate in the power of the Holy Spirit. You don't desire sin; you desire to do what God's Word says.

So remember — it's good for you to desire, as long as it is within the boundaries of God's Word. God wants you to follow Abraham's example by desiring what He has already promised you and acting on your desire in faith. That's when He can bring His promises to pass in your life!

Chapter 2

We Walk by Faith, *Not* by Obstacles

Hope deferred maketh the heart sick: but when the desire cometh, it is a tree of life.

— Proverbs 13:12

Several years ago, I developed a strong desire to become a chaplain in the military. But when I began trying to reach that goal, I faced nothing but obstacles, barriers, and barricades. It seemed like the whole world was against the realization of my heart's desire.

I filled out a multiple-page application. I had to get an endorsement from the denomination through which I would serve. I had to get recommendations from three pastors and from current army officers. I had to get fingerprinted. I had to get a blood test, EKG, urinalysis, and a complete physical.

This process took several weeks to accomplish. I finally got it all done and mailed my application to the recruiter. He received the application, and everything seemed fine — that is, until he lost it. And I had been too ignorant to make copies!

The goal I desired had to be deferred, and it made my heart sick. I wanted to bite someone. I wanted to pull my hair out. I was so sickened by the thought of losing that entire application!

Let's Try Again

So I filled out another multiple-page application. I had to get another endorsement from the denomination. I had to get new recommendations from three pastors and from current army officers. I had to get finger-printed all over again. I had to get another blood test, EKG, urinalysis, and a complete physical. This process took several weeks to accomplish. I finally got it all done and mailed it to the recruiter. He received the application.

However, at that time the recruiting office was located in a Washington D.C. building that was getting rewired for new computer systems. As a part of the rewiring process, furniture was getting moved all around the various offices in the building.

Someone moved the filing cabinet that contained my application out of the recruiting office. When the rewiring process was completed and everything was being put back in place, no one could find the filing cabinet. They had lost the filing cabinet with my application!

The goal I desired was once more deferred, and it made my heart sick. I wanted to bite someone. I wanted to pull my hair out. I was so sickened by the thought of losing that entire application again!

Try and Try Again!

So I filled out another multiple-page application. I had to get another endorsement from the denomination. I had to get new recommendations from three pastors and from current army officers. I had to get fingerprinted all over again. I had to get another blood test, EKG, urinalysis, and a complete physical. This process took several weeks to accomplish. I finally got it all done and mailed it to the recruiter. He received the application.

This time all the officers on the review board flew in from around the country to choose the new chaplains. In this selection process, each officer reviews the applications and then initials his approval.

When the officers took a lunch break, my application was lying in the center of the table with only half the initials necessary for approval. After returning from lunch, the officers forgot where they had left off and started with a new application.

In the end, all the chaplaincy applicants were approved except me. I was not disapproved, but my packet was incomplete because not everyone on the panel had initialed it. And, of course, all the officers weren't going to fly back in just so they could get one incomplete application finished!

The goal I desired was once more deferred, and it made my heart sick. I wanted to bite someone. I wanted to pull my hair out. I was so sickened by the thought of my application not making it through the entire review board!

Do Obstacles Mean
You're Out of God's Will?

A friend said, "Can't you see what's happening? If you are having all these problems, it isn't God's will for you to be a chaplain."

I don't know where my friend got that idea, but it wasn't the Bible. Think about how foolish that human way of thinking is. Just because the wind is blowing a little too hard, that means it's not God's will for you to go out and do what is on your heart to do. Just because you face obstacles, that means it's not His will for you to continue in the direction you're going.

I don't believe God is stupid. Do you? If He wanted us to be led by obstacles, He would have said, "As many as are led by obstacles, they are the sons of God" or "As many as are led by the wind, they are the sons of God." He would have said, "We walk by obstacles and not by faith" or "We walk by the storms of life and not by faith." He would have told us, "For the just shall live according to obstacles" or "The just shall live by negative circumstances."

No! Just because you encounter barriers, obstacles, or storms on the journey is no reason to give up and quit. And it sure doesn't mean it isn't God's will for you to pursue the goal you desire! The Apostle Paul said, *"Wherefore we would have come unto you...but Satan hindered us"* (1 Thess. 2:18). He also said that when God opens a door of opportunity for us, there are many adversaries (1 Cor. 16:9).

In my case, I wanted to quit. When I heard that my application was the only one that hadn't been approved, I immediately thought, *Three strikes and I'm out. I should just give up on my desire.* But my desire was strong enough to keep me going.

So I continued to pursue my goal. In order to become a chaplain, I had to earn a bachelor degree. This took time to accomplish. Colleges don't just give out degrees as free samples at Sam's Club! I had to go after my desire. I couldn't just sit around and wish that it would come. I had to do something about it. I had to do something about it for four years of my life.

In order to become a chaplain, I also had to earn a master of divinity degree. This also took time to accomplish. Colleges don't just give those away either! I had to go after my desire. I couldn't just sit around and wish that it would come. I had to do something about it — for three more years of my life.

In addition, in order to become a chaplain, I had to be ordained for two years. This took time to accomplish as well. They don't sell ordinations at the mall! I had to go after my desire. I couldn't just sit around and wish that it would come. I had to do something about it for two years of my life while I was in graduate school.

Fulfilled Desire Is Sweet

The goal I desired was finally accomplished, and it was sweet to my life. By that, I mean it was sweet to my marriage. It was sweet to my finances. It was sweet to my ministry opportunities. It was sweet to my self-esteem.

PROVERBS 13:19
19 The desire accomplished is sweet to the soul....

The same is true for you. When you accomplish your desire, it makes you feel good about your life. In so many ways, it is sweet to your life.

PROVERBS 19:22
22 The desire of a man is his kindness: and a poor man is better than a liar.

The word "kindness" in this verse means *to bring favor, grace, and benefits*.[2] When you walk by faith until you accomplish the desire God has placed in your heart, that desire will bring you favor. It will bring you grace. It will bring you benefits. It will bring kindness to every area of your life!

---

[2] James Strong, *The Exhaustive Concordance of the Bible* (Peabody, Massachusetts: Hendrickson, 1898), 41.

CHAPTER 3

Lessons in Desire

Let's look at a few examples of people in the Bible who desired something from God. These examples can teach us something about the power of positive desire.

JOHN 5:5-9

5 And a certain man was there, which had an infirmity thirty and eight years.

6 When Jesus saw him lie, and knew that he had been now a long time in that case, he saith unto him, WILT THOU BE MADE WHOLE? [Do you desire to be made whole?]

7 The impotent man answered him, Sir, I have no man, when the water is troubled, to put me into the pool: but while I am coming, another steppeth down before me.

8 Jesus saith unto him, Rise, take up thy bed, and walk.

9 And immediately the man was made whole, and took up his bed, and walked: and on the same day was the sabbath.

There's no doubt that this miracle at the pool of Bethesda was a supernatural move of the Holy Spirit. But Jesus still asked the man, *"Do you desire to be made whole?"*

How Great Is Your Desire?

How badly do you want or desire *your* goal? You see, I have prayed for sick people who I later found out didn't want to get healed because they would stop receiving the government check every month. I know of other people who got healed but didn't want to work, so the sickness came back on them.

Is *your* desire strong enough to obey God? For example, is your desire to get out of debt strong enough to make you willing to cut up your credit cards, if that's what you need to do? Is your desire to be healthy strong enough to make you willing to exercise regularly and start eating right?

Is your desire to pursue a particular career strong enough to make you decide to go to night school instead of watch television every night? Is your desire to play skillfully on your musical instrument strong enough to cause you to start practicing every night? Is your desire to know God strong enough to cause you to read your Bible and commune with Him every day?

Just how badly do you want your heart's desire, whatever that desire may be?

Cleansing of the Leper

In Matthew 8, we read of a man afflicted with leprosy whose desire to be healed was so great, it drove him to the feet of Jesus.

MATTHEW 8:1-3
1 When he was come down from the mountain, great multitudes followed him.
2 And, behold, there came a leper and worshipped him, saying, Lord, if thou wilt [desire], thou canst make me clean.

3 And Jesus put forth his hand, and touched him, saying, I will [desire]; be thou clean. And immediately his leprosy was cleansed.

This man's desire to be healed was strong enough to cause him to act on his faith that Jesus could heal him. However, he still wasn't sure Jesus *wanted* to heal him.

So the man with leprosy said to Jesus, "If You desire to do it, You can make me clean." The man asked Jesus for something according to the will and desire of God. He asked for something inside the boundaries of God's Word. Therefore, Jesus responded, "I desire the same thing you do; be cleansed."

You Receive What You Believe

Let's look at another biblical example of someone who pursued his desire God's way and therefore received his answer.

MATTHEW 8:5
5 And when Jesus was entered into Capernaum, there came unto him a centurion, BESEECHING him.

Notice that word "beseeching." I have never heard anyone say that word in a modern-day conversation, so I looked up the word "beseech" in the dictionary. It means *to earnestly desire.*

Notice what — or better yet, *who* — this centurion was earnestly desiring. He desired *Him* — Jesus. The man was not earnestly desiring to watch four hours of television. He was not earnestly desiring to spend all his time on the internet. He was not earnestly desiring immorality or drug abuse. He was not earnestly desiring alcohol. He was not earnestly desiring to party. He was not earnestly desiring the lust of the flesh, the lust of the eyes, or the pride of life. He was earnestly desiring *Him*. He desired that Jesus would give him the healing power of His Word.

MATTHEW 8:6-13
6 And saying, Lord, my servant lieth at home sick of the palsy, grievously tormented.
7 And Jesus saith unto him, I will come and heal him.
8 The centurion answered and said, Lord, I am not worthy that thou shouldest come under my roof: but speak the word only, and my servant shall be healed.
9 For I am a man under authority, having soldiers under me: and I say to this man, Go, and he goeth; and to another, Come, and he cometh; and to my servant, Do this, and he doeth it.
10 When Jesus heard it, he marvelled, and said to them that followed, Verily I say unto you, I have not found so great faith, no, not in Israel.
11 And I say unto you, That many shall come from the east and west [literally, that within every nation of the earth, people will get born again], **and shall sit down with Abraham, and Isaac, and Jacob, in the kingdom of heaven.**
12 But the children of the kingdom [people of this worldly kingdom who are not born again] **shall be cast out into outer darkness: there shall be weeping and gnashing of teeth.**
13 And Jesus said unto the centurion, Go thy way; and as thou hast believed, so be it done unto thee. And his servant was healed in the selfsame hour.

This centurion got what he desired because he met the divine qualifications. First, he earnestly desired Jesus. He just wanted the Word. Second, he admitted he didn't deserve it. He told Jesus, "I'm not worthy that You should come under my roof." The truth is, the only thing that can make a person worthy to receive God's blessings is faith in the blood of Jesus Christ.

Third, the centurion believed the Word of God. Jesus said, "Go your way; as you have believed, so be it done unto you." The man could have believed that his servant would eventually die — and that is what he would have received. But he believed that his servant would be healed. Jesus said that the centurion would get what he believed, and he did!

Jesus is saying the same thing to all of us who come to Him as the centurion did. Jesus is no respecter of persons. And He is the same yesterday, today, and forever (Heb. 13:8). All we have to do is earnestly desire Him; admit that it is by His grace and not by our works; and believe the Word of God. When we meet these divine qualifications, He says the same thing to us: *"Go your way; as you have believed, so be it done unto you."*

The Desire of the Canaanite Woman

Now let's see what the Canaanite woman who came to Jesus for help can teach us about the power of godly desire.

MATTHEW 15:22
22 And, behold, a woman of Canaan came out of the same coasts, and cried unto him, saying, Have mercy on me, O Lord, thou Son of David; my daughter is grievously vexed with a devil.

As you read this account, it's important to understand that your child doesn't get demon-possessed just by walking down the street. If you take your children to church on Sunday, pray with them every day, and teach them the Word daily, they aren't going to suddenly become possessed by a demon. That just doesn't happen.

But it's a different story if you're out in the world living in sin, partying all the time, and coming home drunk with a different sex partner every night. Some people do that to their children, subjecting them to alcohol, drugs, and witchcraft. They expose their children to every kind of demon the world has to offer. It's no wonder some children become demon-possessed!

The Canaanite people were evil. They prostituted their young girls with strangers and travelers. They practiced open pornography — sexual acts on stage for people to watch. They were involved in child pornography, incest, bestiality, cannibalism, and other savage acts. They acted worse than dogs!

This woman's daughter did not get demon-possessed by going to church three nights a week. The family was not worshiping the true God in their home, so the door was wide open in their lives for a devil to come in and possess the child!

The next verse shows us Jesus' response to the woman's plea for help:

MATTHEW 15:23
23 But he answered her not a word. And his disciples came and besought him, saying, Send her away; for she crieth after us.

Did you know that you can go to Jesus and not receive an immediate answer? Remember, Jesus is the same yesterday, today, and forever. This lady cried as she asked Him to help her daughter, and He still ignored her. Therefore, just because you are sad and depressed — just because you go to Jesus in tears — doesn't necessarily mean He will answer you either. He may want to locate your heart first.

MATTHEW 15:24
24 But he answered and said, I am not sent but unto the lost sheep of the house of Israel.

It was difficult for a Canaanite to listen to a Jew. The Canaanite people didn't like the Jews.

There are some people who can't listen and learn from someone who is not of their own ethnic background. For instance, some Italians, Irish, or Germans can't receive from a Jew. Just the thought of a Jew makes them angry. Some people can't learn from a Hispanic person. Some people can't learn from a black man or a white man.

But God can speak into your life through anyone He chooses — no matter what color that person is! In fact, Numbers 22:28 tells us that He'll speak through a donkey if He has to in order to get His message across to someone!

MATTHEW 15:25,26
25 Then came she and worshipped him, saying, Lord, help me.
26 But he answered and said, It is not meet to take the children's bread, and to cast it to dogs.

Think about this woman's commitment to her desire to see her daughter set free. First, Jesus wouldn't even answer her when she came to Him crying and begging. She humiliated herself to a Jew, and still He ignored her. Many people would have gotten angry and left right then, but the Canaanite woman stayed.

Second, Jesus said, "...*I am not sent but unto the lost sheep of the house of Israel*" (v. 24). Many people would have gotten angry and left at this response. Some would have said, "We're Canaanites. We're better than the Jews!" But this woman stayed and gave no angry retort.

Third, Jesus called this woman a *dog*. Many would have given Jesus a piece of their minds when they heard this. Some would have told Him, "I don't know who You think You are, Jesus! I came all the way over here and embarrassed myself in front of all these people, and still You ignored me. Who do You think You are? Then I fall down and worship You, and You say that You're sent only to the lost Jews. And then You call me a dog! Who are You calling a *dog*? I'm nobody's dog! Do You want a piece of me? Let me tell You something, preacher..." And as they continued to rant and rave, they would have missed out on the blessing Jesus wanted them to receive.

But this Canaanite woman didn't do that. She stayed. She was committed to pursuing her desire. She was committed to the One who could help her. So instead of reacting in anger, she continued to humble herself.

MATTHEW 15:27
27 And she said, Truth, Lord: yet the dogs eat of the crumbs which fall from their masters' table.

In essence, the woman was saying, "You're right, Lord. I have been acting like a dog. I have made so many mistakes, Jesus, but just give me the crumbs so my daughter can be set free."

MATTHEW 15:28
28 Then Jesus answered and said unto her, O woman, great is thy faith: be it unto thee even as thou wilt. And her daughter was made whole from that very hour.

The Canaanite woman stayed committed to her desire. When she could have chosen to react in pride and anger, she chose to respond in humility and faith. And in the end, Jesus gave her the response her heart longed for: *"O woman, great is your faith! Be it unto you even as you desire."* The woman left with her desire fulfilled, for *"...her daughter was made whole from that very hour"*!

The Perseverance
Of Blind Bartimaeus

The blind man Bartimaeus was an example of someone who persevered in the face of opposition until he received his desire.

MARK 10:46-48
46 And they came to Jericho: and as he went out of Jericho with his disciples and a great number of people, blind Bartimaeus, the son of Timaeus, sat by the highway side begging.
47 And when he heard that it was Jesus of Nazareth, he began to cry out, and say, Jesus, thou Son of David, have mercy on me.

48 And many charged him that he should hold his peace: but he cried the more a great deal, Thou son of David, have mercy on me.

You may have been taught by bad religion to accept what life has dealt you. You may have friends who tell you, "Just settle for what you have right now. Don't desire anything better. Just hush up and settle for second best." Your relatives or your church may tell you, "Don't go for it." But just stay focused and thrust forward toward your desire anyway!

Tradition told Bartimaeus to sit there as a blind beggar day after day, week after week, month after month. His religion told him to sit there and suffer for God. Everyone in Bartimaeus' world — his friends, his community, his church, the crowd following Jesus — told him that he couldn't have his sight, the thing he desired most. But still he pressed in. He didn't listen to negative friends. He didn't listen to unbelieving relatives. He didn't listen to the crowd telling him to hush and settle for mediocrity.

People will tell you that you can't *do* what you desire; you can't *have* what you desire; you can't *be* what you desire. But rise up and go for it anyway! Don't listen to voices of doubt and unbelief, whether they come from your church, your relatives, your community, or your friends.

MARK 10:48-50
48 And many charged him that he should hold his peace: but he cried the more a great deal, Thou son of David, have mercy on me.

49 And Jesus stood still, and commanded him to be called. And they call the blind man, saying unto him, Be of good comfort, rise; he calleth thee.
50 And he, casting away his garment, rose, and came to Jesus.

Bartimaeus threw off that old garment of compromise, complacency, and mediocrity. He threw off that old garment of man's tradition and dead religion. He threw off that old garment of unbelief, fear, and doubt — the garment everyone else wanted him to wear.

Then Bartimaeus rose up! He rose above what the crowd said. He rose above those voices of unbelief. He rose above the tradition. He rose above the dead religion. He rose above the philosophy of man. He rose above manmade doctrines and dogmas. *He rose up to receive what he desired!*

You can do the same thing. Rise up and take what belongs to you within the boundaries of God!

It makes no difference what your situation is. It doesn't matter how old or how young you are. It doesn't matter what color your skin is or what gender you are. It doesn't matter how much money you have. It doesn't matter what circumstances you may be facing. You can do it! Press on, press in, and receive what God wants you to have!

It also doesn't matter how many mistakes you've made or how many failures you've experienced. Think back to Abraham's life. Abraham made mistakes, but he would not quit. He failed at times, but he would not give up. He pressed on toward the desire God had given him.

The next two verses tell us the outcome of
Bartimaeus' tenacious pursuit of his desire:

MARK 10:51,52
**51 And Jesus answered and said unto him,
WHAT WILT THOU THAT I SHOULD DO UNTO
THEE? The blind man said unto him, Lord, that
I might receive my sight.**
**52 And Jesus said unto him, Go thy way; thy
faith hath made thee whole. And immediately
he received his sight, and followed Jesus in the
way.**

When you go after God's desire for you with the
same kind of perseverance Bartimaeus had, Jesus says
the same thing to you: *"What do you desire that I do for
you? Great is your faith; be it unto you even as you
desire."*

CHAPTER 4

Receive What You Desire!

Therefore I say unto you, What things soever ye desire, when ye pray, believe that ye receive them, and ye shall have them.

— Mark 11:24

There is a time frame between the moment you believe you receive your desire and the moment you actually see it materialize in front of your face. You already have it when you believe you receive it, but you have to press on until you see it materialize in this natural realm.

The word "ye" in Mark 11:24 means *you*. Notice that the word "you" is used five times in this verse. The verse is talking to *you*. Whatever *you* desire. When *you* pray. Believe that *you* receive them, and *you* shall have them. What is "them" referring to? It is referring to the desires that you believe you receive.

Abide in God's Desire
For You

So how do you press on between the *prayer* of faith and the manifested *promise*? Jesus tells you in John 15:

JOHN 15:7
7 If ye abide in me, and my words abide in you, ye shall ask what ye will [desire], and it shall be done unto you.

Abide in Jesus. Abide in His boundaries. Abide in His desire. Abide in His plan for your life. Don't live anywhere but under the umbrella of faith.

Keep putting His Word on the inside of you until it is living and abiding in you. Plant His desires and His plan in your heart until they are living and abiding in you. Then you can ask Him for whatever you desire. Because you don't desire anything outside of His boundaries or His desire, Jesus promises that you *will* receive. He didn't say, "Well, you might not get it." He said, *"It shall be done unto you."*

Do you want the Father to be glorified through you? The Father receives glory when you abide in Him and within His boundaries. He receives glory when you put His Word in your heart. He is glorified when you ask Him in faith for what you desire. He is glorified when you receive the desires of your heart.

Does God Supply Wants?

When I was working on my master's degree, I met a minister who became a close friend. One day he said, "I've been in the ministry for over twenty years, and I've never seen anywhere in the Bible where God says something about our wants."

I said, "I have! Psalm 23:1 says, *'The Lord is my shepherd; I shall not want.'* And what about Psalm 34:9 and 10? *'O fear the Lord, ye his saints: for there is no want to them that fear him. The young lions do lack, and suffer hunger: but they that seek the Lord shall not want any good thing.'* Then Paul said, *'For the administration of this service* [sowing and reaping] *not only supplieth the want of the saints, but is abundant also by many thanksgivings unto God'* (2 Cor. 9:12)."

That discussion prompted my friend and me to study the Word together on the subject. By the time we had finished our study, my friend concluded that God will supply to the full all our *need, lack,* or *want* according to His riches in glory!

First Desire —
Then Receive

You will never *have* anything until you first desire it. You will never *be* anything until you first desire it. You will never *do* anything until you first desire it.

You will never give what you have to God's plan until you want to. You will never be born again until you first desire salvation enough to lay hold of it. You will never receive the infilling of the Holy Spirit with the evidence of speaking in tongues until you first desire that gift enough to lay hold of it.

You will never receive and keep your healing until you first desire it enough to lay hold of it. You will never receive prosperity and success until you first desire it and then lay claim to it. You will never receive a higher education until you first desire it enough to pursue it. You will never be in the ministry until you first desire it and then do your part. You will never have a wife or husband until you first desire one enough to actively prepare for marriage and believe God for your mate.

You will never learn another language until you desire it enough to study. You will never learn how to play a musical instrument until you desire it enough to practice. You will never live a debt-free life until you desire it strongly enough to stop filling up your credit card with more debt. You will never have a better career until you desire it enough to do something to improve your skills. You will never do missions work until you desire it enough to go for it.

You will never achieve your desires until you do something about them.

God wants you to know that it isn't wrong to desire to progress. It isn't wrong to desire to prosper. It isn't wrong to desire to produce fruit for the Kingdom of God. It isn't wrong to desire to be promoted to success-ful living. If Jesus came so we could have more abun-dant life, we were born to enjoy all the blessings of this life.

A common distinction of people who are victorious in life is that they deeply desire.[3] They *concentrate* on what they desire. They don't quit when things get tough. They face obstacles, but they are committed to making it through. They disregard any excuses and limitations they may encounter. They stay within the boundaries of God and go for the dream God has given them.

Time To Take Inventory

You can be anything you want to be. You can do anything you want to do. You can have anything you want to have through Christ's love plan for your life — *if* you desire it enough to go after it in faith.

---

[3] T. L. Osborn, *Go for It,* 75.

Desire is a basic fundamental of faith. It is essential to faith. There *is* no faith without desire. You cannot please God without desire.

You have a right to please God; therefore, you have a right to desire. Whatever things you desire when you pray, believe that you receive them, and you will have them. I challenge you to desire God's desire. I dare you to desire His promises of abundant provision and wonderful life through Christ!

God desires for you to be in health and prosperity — spirit, soul, and body. He said, *"Beloved, I wish above all things that thou mayest prosper and be in health, even as thy soul prospereth"* (3 John 1:2). What's more, it gives God pleasure to see you fulfilled. Therefore, if you desire to be fulfilled in every area of your life, you must realize that this is God's desire being expressed in you.

So take some time to do some inventory in your heart. What do you want out of life more than anything else — I mean, with your whole heart and soul? What do you truly, deeply desire? If it is holy, right, and good and if God has approved it, then your desire is also what *He* desires for you.

Make the decision to desire more than the average person settles for. If you are hooked up to God, there is no limit to your fulfillment. It is up to you. Don't be afraid! Desire the good things of life God has for you! Go for it!

The Father has waited since before the foundations of the earth for His desire to be fulfilled in your life. So give Him glory by acting out His desire. Lay aside all religious traditions, human philosophies, and fleshly fear. Grab hold of your desire for God's plan for your life. Hold fast to it with every ounce of your faith. As you do, you'll see that divine plan start unfolding in your life right before your eyes!

Don't Settle for Less Than God Has for You

One of the greatest sins you can do is settle for nothing.[4] It's your choice. You can refuse to use what God has provided. You can refuse to discipline yourself to develop and expand. You can refuse to apply and practice the necessary skills. You can refuse to sharpen yourself toward your desires. You can choose to sit back and wait until you die. But if that's what you decide to do, you'll get to Heaven and say, "I wish I would have."[5]

The late Abraham Joshua Heschel, the great Jewish theologian, said that a failure to educate your desire brings with it an impulse to suppress it.[6] He also said that for a Jew to escape his desire rushes him or her to corruption.[7] Heschel was saying that nothing good comes out of eliminating your desire. From the Hebrew perspective, God does not require His people to give up the right to desire.

To ask someone to give up his desire is to ask him to give up his life. If giving up one's life were the ultimate virtue, the logical conclusion would be that people should all kill themselves. Suicide would be the ultimate moral decision!

---

[4] T. L. Osborn, *Go for It,* 79.
[5] T. L. Osborn, *Go for It,* 79.
[6] Abraham Joshua Heschel, *A Philosophy of Judaism* (New York: Noonday Press, 1955), 398.
[7] Abraham Joshua Heschel, *A Philosophy of Judaism,* 398.

The prophets of Baal were examples of those who ruined themselves by giving up all desire. Many man-made religions of the world require suppression and indulge in self-mortification. For example, asceticism says that one must seek to restrict or restrain oneself from, deny, or give up anything enjoyable that may prove a hindrance to the cultivation of one's spiritual life.[8]

Also, Gnostics taught that the created order was evil, inferior, and opposed to the good. Therefore, since man's body and soul are part of his earthly existence, they are evil. Gnostics believed that salvation comes when the spirit, the divine substance of man that is asleep and ignorant, is awakened and liberated by knowledge. Thus, Gnostics tended to treat their bodies austerely, suppressing their natural desires in an attempt to separate themselves from the evil of this earthly realm.[9]

But the truth is, a person who endeavors to give up all desire is only providing himself an occasion to return to bondage. In a sense, he has embarked on a suicidal "kamikaze" mission that will end in his own destruction.

Setting the Record Straight

I want to specifically point out two important areas of life that God designed for His people to desire. In general, Jewish people understand their right to desire in these areas. However, many world religions try to

---

[8] Marvin R. Wilson, *Our Father Abraham* (Grand Rapids, Michigan: W. B. Eerdmans Publishing Company, 1989), 169.
[9] *Nelson's Illustrated Bible Dictionary* (Nashville: Thomas Nelson Publishers, 1986).

deny people their ability to desire and enjoy these blessings.

First, let's look at the financial realm of life. It's all right for God's people to desire to increase in their finances, as long as they stay within the boundaries of His Word. Since poverty is a curse, God's people should not desire the curse (*see* Deut. 28:1-14).

We should desire the blessings of God, which include material and financial prosperity. In fact, what we really ought to do is take a vow of *prosperity*, not of poverty! If we are willing (desiring) and obedient, we will *eat* the good of the land, *drive* the good of the land, *wear* the good of the land, and *live* in the good of the land (Isa. 1:19)!

So get willing. Start desiring God's plan of abundance and prosperity for your life. You see, your work, your gift, your life, and your contribution is accepted when you are doing it out of a heart desire (2 Cor. 8:3).

2 CORINTHIANS 8:14
14 For if there be first a willing [desiring] **mind, it is accepted according to that a man hath....**

EPHESIANS 6:6
6 Not with eyeservice, as menpleasers; but as the servants of Christ, doing the will [desire] **of God from the heart.**

Second, let's talk about man's sexual desires. It's all right to desire sex as long as it is within the boundaries of marriage. God created sex for pleasure. He created humans with sexual desire. Again, Jewish people believe sex is a blessing that married couples should enjoy for more than just the purpose of child-bearing. However, some world religions deny people the right to desire this blessing and, as a result, keep them unhappy and unfulfilled.

Surrender to God's Desire

We all need to surrender to the desire and will of God. When we surrender, He is able to work in us both to will (desire) and to do of His good pleasure (Phil. 2:13).

In order to surrender to God's desire, you must pray as Jesus taught His disciples to pray: *"Thy kingdom come. Thy will be done in earth, as it is in heaven"* (Matt. 6:10). God desires for Heaven and earth to be filled with His glory, peace, health, happiness, and prosperity. He wants you to live a rich and fulfilled life. So surrender to what pleases God. After you have done the *will* of God, you shall receive the promise.

You might be asking, "But how can I know God's will for my life?" Surrender to the Word daily. Renew your mind with the Word of God. This is how you learn what He wants. He has accepted you according to the good pleasure of His *will*. As you continually feed on the Word, you will come to know the good, acceptable, and perfect will or desire of God for your life (Rom. 12:2).

You will learn what He wants for your marriage. For instance, in First Thessalonians 4:3, it says, *"For this is the will of God, even your sanctification, that ye should abstain from fornication."* Just as we discussed earlier, sex is a God-given desire, but not outside of marriage.

You will learn what God wants for your body and for your finances. For instance, the Apostle John said,

"Beloved, I wish above all things that thou mayest prosper and be in health, even as thy soul prospereth" (3 John 1:2). God wants you healthy and wealthy.

You will learn what God wants for your children. Ephesians 6:1-3 says, *"Children, obey your parents in the Lord: for this is right. Honour thy father and mother... That it may be well with thee, and thou mayest live long on the earth."* God's plan for your children is obedience, wellness, and long life.

You will learn what God wants for your attitude. For instance, First Thessalonians 5:18 says, *"In every thing give thanks: for this is the will of God in Christ Jesus concerning you."* God wants you to always be thankful.

You will learn what God wants for your eternity. For instance, Second Peter 3:9 says that God is *"...not willing that any should perish, but that all should come to repentance."* He wants you to spend eternity in Heaven with Him.

So pray like Jesus prayed in the Garden of Gethsemane: *"...Abba, Father, all things are possible unto thee...nevertheless not what I will, but what thou wilt"* (Mark 14:36). Surrender to what God desires.

Do you want to mature spiritually and walk worthy before the Lord? Then walk in the desire of God. When you surrender to Him, He will make you mature in every good work to do His will (desire), working in you that which is well pleasing in His sight (Heb. 13:21).

Paul prayed for the Colossians, saying, *"For this cause we also, since the day we heard it, do not cease to pray for you, and to desire that ye might be filled with the knowledge of his will* [desire] *in all wisdom and spiritual understanding; That ye might walk worthy of the Lord unto all pleasing, being fruitful in every good work, and increasing in the knowledge of God"* (Col. 1:9,10). That same prayer applies to you and me as well. We will please God by living out His desire for us.

Epaphras also fervently labored in prayer for the Colossians that they would stand perfect and complete in all the will (desire) of God (Col. 4:12).

Heschel said that desire is the father of what is valuable.[10] Just think about what proper desire leads to:

- Desire leads to originality.
- Desire leads to inventions.
- Desire leads to ingenuity.
- Desire leads to creativity.
- Desire leads to new discovery.
- Desire leads to better development.
- Desire leads to better resourcefulness.
- Desire leads to better skills and quality work.
- Desire leads to better work environments.
- Desire leads to better water supplies and new roads.
- Desire leads to better transportation: planes, trains, and automobiles.
- Desire leads to better communication: video, cable internet, pagers, cellular phones, and satellite television.
- Desire leads to better housing and better lifestyles.

---

[10] Abraham Joshua Heschel, *A Philosophy of Judaism*, 396.

Take Hold of God's Best
For You!

How do we please God? Faith pleases God (Heb. 11:6). But without desire, there is no faith. There is no way to please God without desiring.

Your prayers will not be answered unless you *desire* that for which you are believing God. Remember, Mark 11:24 says, *"Therefore I say unto you, What things soever ye desire, when ye pray, believe that ye receive them, and ye shall have them."*

God is waiting for you to dare to desire His plan of happiness and fulfillment. The next move is yours. I challenge you to commit to the desire of your heart. It will never actualize until you do something.

God is waiting on you, so get fired up about your desire! It is a God-given plan. It is His dream and His purpose at work on the inside of you. You not only please Him, but you find fulfillment for yourself when you pursue the desire He has placed in your heart.

The time is now. You can advance. You can take hold of the best God has for you. You can have what you want to have. You can do what you want to do. You can be what you want to be. But you will only do it through the power of positive desire!

Bibliography

Heschel, Abraham Joshua. *A Philosophy of Judaism.* New York: Noonday Press, 1955.

Nelson's Illustrated Bible Dictionary. Nashville: Thomas Nelson Publishers, 1986.

Osborn, T. L. *Go for It! Get the Best Out of Life.* Tulsa: Osborn Books, 1983.

Strong, James. *The Exhaustive Concordance of the Bible.* Peabody, Massachusetts: Hendrickson, 1898.

Wilson, Marvin R. *Our Father Abraham.* Grand Rapids, Michigan: W. B. Eerdmans Publishing Company, 1989.

For additional copies of this book
or for further information
regarding Rev. Hernandez's ministry schedule,
please write:

Rev. Joe F. Hernandez
811 Woodmeadow Place
Oakley, CA 94561